Parks of Sapporo, Japan

A TRAVEL PHOTO ART BOOK

LAINE CUNNINGHAM

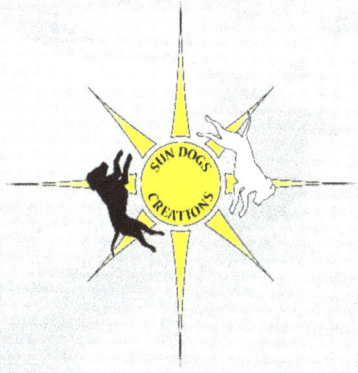

Parks of Sapporo, Japan

A Travel Photo Art Book

Published by Sun Dogs Creations
Changing the World One Book at a Time
Print ISBN: 978-1-951389-30-7

Cover Images by Laine Cunningham
Cover Design by Angel Leya

Copyright © 2023 Laine Cunningham

All rights reserved. No part of this book may be reproduced in any form or by any means, electronic, mechanical, digital, photocopying or recording, except for the inclusion in a review, without permission in writing from the publisher.

Sapporo, in the Hokkaido prefecture, is located on Japan's second-largest island. It also is the northernmost large city. The city's parks allow visitors to enjoy many of the region's unique natural attractions just by traveling a few metro stops.

Nakajima Park, for example, is a sprawling downtown area next to the Susukino shopping district. Hokkaido University's botanical garden changes with the seasons, and functions as a nature preserve. Tenjinyama Ryokuchi Park provides arts-related activities to the public. Tsukisamu Park, like so many other of Sapporo's parks, contains a playground for the younger crowds as well as adult sports facilities.

The richness of the Hokkaido region is never more than a few minutes away. Take a break from the busy city streets by slipping through one of these green oases. Linger long enough for a picnic, visit the shrines inside many of the parks, or let the kids play on the colorful equipment. Whether you're a birdwatcher or a plant lover, Sapporo's parks are waiting to welcome you.

MOAI

DOROTHY RETURNS

CURIOUS

EMBROIDERED

BEACON

REGAL

PIECEMEAL

PERSIST

EVERGLADES

WEDDING MARCH

PAIRED

UNBOUND

FUZZ

BELUGA

WHEELING

HARDSCAPING

PATCHES

STABLE

EMBRACE

HUSH

YOKE

GLIDE

CURVATURE

CANDIED

GRACE

SLATE

CLOISTER

MEANDER

GOLDEN MEAN

MOODY

ROUNDABOUT

SPLASH

PREPARATIONS

COMPOSED

APPROACH

PASSAGE

GATHERING

MUGWORT

EXPANSION

ENTER

POPSTARS

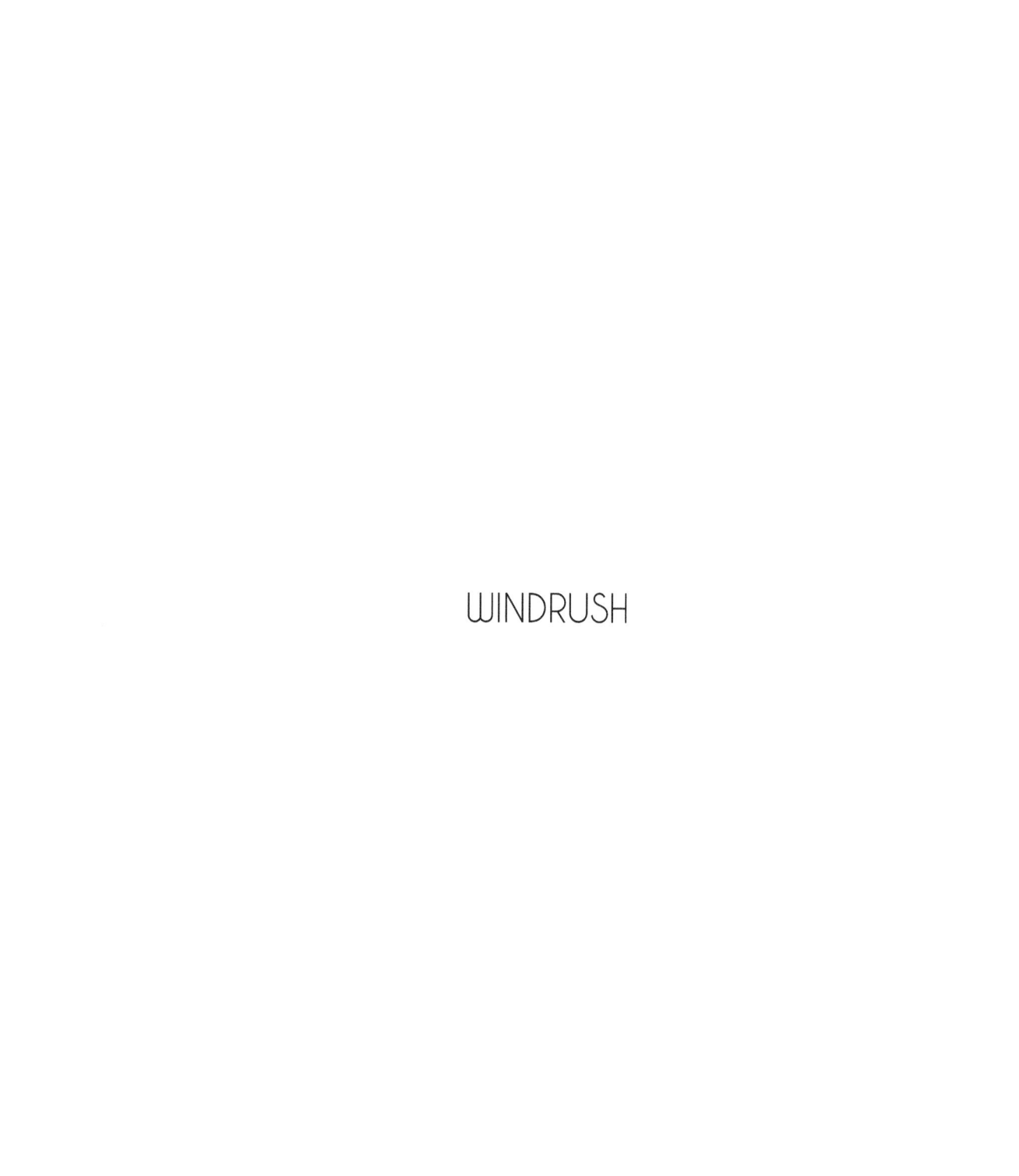

SWIMMING

TITLES IN THIS SERIES

Gardens of Sapporo, Japan
Mt. Moiwa, Sapporo, Japan
Shrines of Sapporo, Japan
Parks of Sapporo, Japan
Sapporo City, Japan

www.ingramcontent.com/pod-product-compliance
Lightning Source LLC
Chambersburg PA
CBHW051359110526
44592CB00023B/2881